◼ SCHOLASTIC

READ & RESPOND

Bringing the best books to life in the classroom

Activities based on **A Christmas Carol** By Charles Dickens

CHARLES DICKENS

A CHRISTMAS CAROL

FOR AGES 7–11

Scholastic Education, an imprint of Scholastic Ltd
Book End, Range Road, Witney, Oxfordshire, OX29 0YD
Registered office: Westfield Road, Southam, Warwickshire CV47 0RA

Printed and bound by Ashford Colour Press
© 2017 Scholastic Ltd
1 2 3 4 5 6 7 8 9   7 8 9 0 1 2 3 4 5 6

British Library Cataloguing-in-Publication Data
A catalogue record for this book is available from the British Library.
ISBN 978-1407-17615-4

Due to the nature of the web, we cannot guarantee the content or links of any site mentioned. We strongly recommend that teachers check websites before using them in the classroom.

Author Eileen Jones
Editorial team Audrey Stokes, Suzanne Adams, Vicki Yates
Series designers Neil Salt and Alice Duggan
Designer Alice Duggan
Illustrator Davide Ortu/Beehive Illustration

Acknowledgements
The publishers gratefully acknowledge permission to reproduce the following copyright material:
Scholastic Children's Books for permission to use the cover from *A Christmas Carol* written by Charles Dickens (Scholastic Children's Books, 2016). Reproduced with permission of Scholastic Children's Books. All rights reserved.

Photographs
page 8: Charles Dickens, Shutterstock

Every effort has been made to trace copyright holders for the works reproduced in this book, and the publishers apologise for any inadvertent omissions.

CONTENTS ▽

How to use Read & Respond in your classroom...

Read & Respond provides teaching ideas related to a specific well-loved children's book. Each Read & Respond book is divided into the following sections:

ABOUT THE BOOK AND AUTHOR

Gives you some background information about the book and the author.

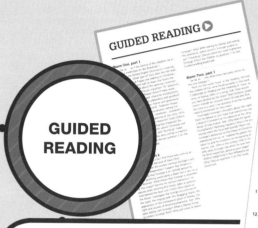

GUIDED READING

Breaks the book down into sections and gives notes for using it with guided reading groups. A bookmark has been provided on page 12 containing comprehension questions. The children can be directed to refer to these as they read.

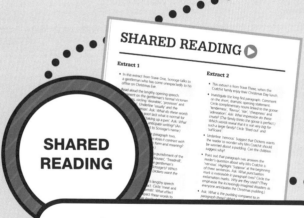

SHARED READING

Provides extracts from the children's book with associated notes for focused work. There is also one non-fiction extract that relates to the children's book.

GRAMMAR, PUNCTUATION & SPELLING

Provides word-level work related to the children's book so you can teach grammar, punctuation and spelling in context.

PLOT, CHARACTER & SETTING

Contains activity ideas focused on the plot, characters and the setting of the story.

GET WRITING

Provides writing activities related to the children's book. These activities may be based directly on the children's book or be broadly based on the themes and concepts of the story.

TALK ABOUT IT

Has speaking and listening activities related to the children's book. These activities may be based directly on the children's book or be broadly based on the themes and concepts of the story.

ASSESSMENT

Contains short activities that will help you assess whether the children have understood concepts and curriculum objectives. They are designed to be informal activities to feed into your planning.

" The titles are great fun to use and cover exactly the range of books that children most want to read. It makes it easy to explore texts fully and ensure the children want to keep on reading more.
Chris Flanagan, Year 5 Teacher, St Thomas of Canterbury Primary School *"*

Activities

The activities follow the same format:

- **Objective:** the objective for the lesson. It will be based upon a curriculum objective, but will often be more specific to the focus being covered.

- **What you need:** a list of resources you need to teach the lesson, including printable pages.

- **What to do:** the activity notes.

- **Differentiation:** this is provided where specific and useful differentiation advice can be given to support and/or extend the learning in the activity. Differentiation by providing additional adult support has not been included as this will be at a teacher's discretion based upon specific children's needs and ability, as well as the availability of support.

The activities are numbered for reference within each section and should move through the text sequentially – so you can use the lesson while you are reading the book. Once you have read the book, most of the activities can be used in any order you wish.

CURRICULUM LINKS

Section	Activity	Curriculum objectives
Guided reading		Comprehension: To predict what might happen from details stated and implied.
Shared reading	1	Comprehension: To discuss and evaluate how writers use language, including figurative language, considering the impact on the reader.
	2	Comprehension: To draw inferences such as inferring characters' feelings, thoughts and motives from their actions, and justifying inferences with evidence.
	3	Comprehension: To check that the book makes sense to them, discussing their understanding and exploring the meaning of words in context.
	4	Comprehension: To continue to read and discuss an increasingly wide range of fiction, poetry, plays, non-fiction and reference or textbooks.
Grammar, punctuation & spelling	1	Vocabulary, grammar and punctuation: To use semi-colons, colons or dashes to mark boundaries between independent clauses.
	2	Transcription: To use suffixes to convert nouns or adjectives into verbs.
	3	Vocabulary, grammar and punctuation: To use passive verbs to affect the presentation of information in a sentence.
	4	Vocabulary, grammar and punctuation: To use commas to clarify meaning or avoid ambiguity in writing.
	5	Spelling: To spell some words with 'silent' letters.
	6	Spelling: To continue to distinguish between homophones and other words which are often confused.
Plot, character & setting	1	Spelling: To continue to distinguish between homophones and other words which are often confused.
	2	Comprehension: To predict what might happen from details stated and implied.
	3	Comprehension: To discuss and evaluate how authors use language...considering the impact on the reader.
	4	Comprehension: To check that the book makes sense to them...exploring the meaning of words in context.
	5	Comprehension: To read books that are structured in different ways.
	6	Comprehension: To identify and discuss themes and conventions in a wide range of writing.
	7	Comprehension: To ask questions to improve their understanding.
	8	Comprehension: To infer characters' feelings, thoughts and motives from their actions.

Section	Activity	Curriculum objectives
Talk about it	1	Spoken language: To participate in discussions...and debates.
	2	Spoken language: To use spoken language to develop understanding through speculating, hypothesising, imagining and exploring ideas.
	3	Spoken language and comprehension: To participate in...role play; to infer characters' feelings, thoughts and motives.
	4	Spoken language: To give well-structured...narratives for different purposes, including for expressing feelings.
	5	Spoken language: To use spoken language to develop understanding through speculating, hypothesising, imagining and exploring ideas.
	6	Spoken language: To participate in...role play; to develop understanding through speculating, hypothesising, imagining and exploring ideas.
Get writing	1	Composition: To identify the audience for and purpose of the writing, selecting the appropriate form and using other similar writing as models for their own.
	2	Composition: To use further organisational and presentational devices to structure text and to guide the reader.
	3	Composition: To assess the effectiveness of their own and others' writing.
	4	Composition: To plan their writing by identifying...the purpose of the writing.
	5	Composition: To note and develop initial ideas.
	6	Composition: To describe settings, characters and atmosphere and integrating dialogue.
Assessment	1	Vocabulary, grammar and punctuation: To use hyphens to avoid ambiguity.
	2	Comprehension: To explore the meaning of words in context.
	3	Composition: To distinguish between the language of speech and writing and choosing the appropriate register.
	4	Comprehension: To identify and discuss themes and conventions across a wide range of writing.
	5	Composition: To note and develop initial ideas.
	6	Comprehension: To recommend books that they have read to their peers, giving reasons for their choices.

Key facts

A Christmas Carol

◉ **Author:**
Charles Dickens

◉ **First published:**
1843 by Chapman & Hall

◉ **Did you know?**
A Christmas Carol proved so popular that it has never been out of print. It has been translated into many languages and has been adapted for stage and film versions.

About the book

A Christmas Carol, a novella written for adults, matches the maturing tastes and literacy curriculum of upper Key Stage 2.

The main character is Scrooge, a miserly, anti-social London banker. His firm is called 'Scrooge and Marley', but his business partner is now dead. Scrooge runs his premises with the sole support of Bob Cratchit, his underpaid, downtrodden clerk. It is Christmas Eve, but Scrooge rejects all advances of merrymaking: he declines his nephew's invitation to Christmas dinner, he refuses to contribute to the traditional City collection for the poor, he chases away an innocent carol singer, and he berates his clerk for wanting Christmas Day at home with his wife and children. In this angry, unseasonal mood, Scrooge reaches his dreary home.

As darkness and fog create an eerie atmosphere, Scrooge is shocked by the face of his deceased partner on his door knocker, but blames his imagination. However, Marley's ghost appears later to warn Scrooge of the eternal misery that awaits him. Scrooge's only hope of avoiding this fate is to be visited by three spirits. Scrooge receives separate visits from the Ghosts of Christmas Past, Present and Future. Each spirit takes him to observe important scenes: his boyhood and youth; the happy, grateful Christmas celebrations being enjoyed by his clerk and nephew; and finally the miserable, unmourned death awaiting the Scrooge whose meanness caused the death of Bob's crippled son, Tiny Tim. Scrooge understands that if he wants to avoid his fate and keep Tiny Tim alive, he must be generous and care about others. On Christmas morning, he awakes a changed man.

About the author

Charles Dickens was born in 1812. He had to leave school aged 12 years to work in a factory when his father was put into prison. On Sundays, Charles used to spend the day with his father at the prison. The fate of people there, and the harsh working conditions of his own ten-hour days at the blacking factory, made a lasting impression on Dickens and later influenced his fiction. Despite his lack of a formal education, he wrote *The Pickwick Papers* in serial form in 1836. Within a few years, Dickens was regarded as an international literary celebrity. His novels were mostly published in weekly or monthly instalments. This was a useful method for Dickens: he could gauge the audience's reaction and adapt his writing accordingly. Other successful works followed, for example *Oliver Twist*, *David Copperfield* and *Great Expectations*. These books reflected life in early Victorian London and exposed the hardships suffered by the poor. Charles Dickens died in 1870.

GUIDED READING ▶

Stave One, part 1

(as far as '...as if the Genius of the Weather sat in mournful meditation on the threshold.')

Refer to the Oxford English Dictionary's meaning of 'carol'. Ask: *What type of story does the title lead you to expect? (*A happy one relating to Christmas.) Suggest that the first half of Stave One forms the story's opening. Talk about the opening's function: to hook the reader. Discuss important 'W' questions. (Who? What? Why? Where? When?) Have some been answered? Point out: character introductions; the subjects of Christmas celebration and goodwill, the conditions of the poor, charity and generosity; London place names ('Cornhill', 'Mansion House', 'St Paul's') and items and vocabulary setting the story in the past ('candles', 'comforter', 'poulterers'). Assess the success of the opening of this story. Who seems likely to be the main character? Does Dickens deliberately sketch an unattractive character? Do Scrooge's extreme comments about Christmas and his miserable words 'Bah!' and 'Humbug!' make the reader wonder how this story will be a cheerful carol? Ask the children to discuss question 2 on the Guided reading bookmark.

Stave One, part 2

(from 'Now, it is a fact that there was nothing at all particular...' to the end of Stave One)

Ask: *Why does the author mention Scrooge's lack of 'fancy' or imagination?* Suggest that Dickens is emphasising that Scrooge is an unlikely person to imagine anything, particularly a dead man's face on a door knocker. *What shows that Scrooge is unsettled by this image?* Identify his nervous behaviour: he pauses when entering the house, takes a cautious look behind the door and checks other places in the house. Investigate the strange occurrences of the night: the ringing bells, the dragging chains, the appearance of the transparent ghost of Marley, the sight and sounds of moaning phantoms. Ask: *Why does Marley visit Scrooge? What is Marley trying to protect Scrooge from? Who will come to haunt*

Scrooge? Why? After talking to Marley and seeing the phantoms, which word is Scrooge unable to say? ('Humbug') Discuss what has most frightened Scrooge. Direct the children to question 1 on the Guided reading bookmark.

Stave Two, part 1

(as far as: '...the other boys had gone home for the jolly holidays.')

Point out the word 'Stave' in the heading. Remind the children of the same heading earlier in the book. Collaborate on finding out the meaning of 'stave' (a verse or stanza, often in a song). Ask: *How would you have divided up the story? Does Dickens' poetic choice indicate an unusual story?* (It indicates that the story is a carol.) Use question 6 on the Guided reading bookmark for discussion.

Investigate Scrooge's thoughts about the night. Does he believe or just hope that everything was a dream? Comment on his pleasure at the 'ding dong' of one o'clock. Ask: *Why does he speak triumphantly?* (Nothing happens.) *How is he proved wrong when the hour bell sounds?* Point out Scrooge's deference to the Ghost of Christmas Past, addressing him as 'sir'. Explore the places Scrooge is taken to and his emotions on recognising childhood scenes. Ask: *Who is the solitary child in the school? Why does Scrooge sob when he sees him? Why does he think regretfully about a carol singer?* Are the children beginning to feel differently about Scrooge? Why? Discuss question 1 on the Guided reading bookmark.

Stave Two, part 2

(from 'He was not reading now, but walking up and down despairingly…' to the end of Stave Two)

Question the children about the boy. Ask: *Did he love his family? Was he happy to be going home with Fan?* Point out that Scrooge feels uneasy when the ghost mentions his nephew. Why? Explore the stages of Scrooge's life. Notice the kindness shown to the young Scrooge as an apprentice clerk. Contrast the mean-spiritedness of the present Scrooge with Fezziwig's Christmas celebration. Ask: *What does Scrooge realise about an employer's power of over his apprentice?* (He is responsible for his happiness.) *Why would Scrooge suddenly like to speak to his clerk?* Investigate the development of avarice as Scrooge ages. Ask: *Why does the girl release him from his former promise? How does Scrooge feel when the ghost forces him to watch Belle in later happiness?* Discuss what Scrooge hears the husband and wife say about him. How do the children think he feels as he listens? Could he be frightened? Ask the children to discuss question 9 on the Guided reading bookmark.

Stave Three, part 1

(as far as '…into the suburbs of the town.')

Point out Scrooge's changed attitude: he believes a second spirit will come and wants to be awake, waiting for him. Ask: *Why does Scrooge tremble? What comes when the clock sounds?* (a light) *Why does Scrooge go into the adjoining room?* Discuss the changed state of the room. Examine the conversation between Scrooge and the Ghost of Christmas Present. Ask: *Why is Scrooge friendlier than he was to the first ghost?* (He knows that the ghosts can teach him.) Comment on the scenes and people that Scrooge is taken to see. Ask: *What is sprinkled on the kind and the poor?* (happiness) Encourage the children to discuss question 5 on the Guided reading bookmark.

Stave Three, part 2

(from 'It was a remarkable quality of the Ghost…' as far as '…and especially on Tiny Tim, until the last.')

Read the early description of this spirit. How does the spirit contrast with the miserly Scrooge? (The spirit is 'good', 'kind', 'generous', 'hearty'.) Ask: *Where do the spirit's good qualities lead him?* (He goes to the Cratchits' house to sprinkle blessings.) *What is emphasised about the Cratchits' clothes, food and appearance?* (They are grateful for little, and enjoy celebrating together at Christmas.) *Where is Martha likely to have been?* (She may work in service.) Discuss what Scrooge may learn from watching the Cratchit family's celebration. Ask: *How is he likely to feel when he hears himself toasted? Why does he keep staring at the family, particularly Tiny Tim? What could he be thinking?* Direct the children to question 9 on the Guided reading bookmark for discussion.

Stave Three, part 3

(from 'By this time it was getting dark…' to the end of Stave Three)

Remind the children of the period in time when Dickens was writing before they answer question 7 on the Guided reading bookmark. Comment on the spirit's speed as he moves Scrooge to new places. What surprises Scrooge in each scene? (There are always happy people, even in miserable situations.) Ask: *Which laugh does Scrooge recognise? What does Fred find so funny?* Explore Fred's views on Scrooge. Ask: *Is he correct in thinking that Scrooge, by rejecting Fred's hospitality, misses out on happiness? Does the watching Scrooge, now enjoying their games, realise this?* Discuss the effect of the toast as Scrooge becomes 'light of heart'. Investigate the final scene, as Scrooge sees the children, Ignorance and Want. Does the mood change? Ask: *What does Scrooge's use of 'refuge' and 'resource' show? Has Scrooge's attitude to people changed?* Point out that the spirit throws Scrooge's early words about 'prisons' and 'workhouses' back at him. Let the children discuss question 10 on the Guided reading bookmark.

Stave Four, part 1

(as far as '…Merciful Heaven, what is this?')

Examine the early pages of this stave. What is strange about the dialogue? (It is one-sided: the 'Phantom' does not answer Scrooge's questions.) Investigate the conversations among Scrooge's business acquaintances. Ask: *What are they talking about? Are there clues to the identity of 'he'?* Comment on the successful businessmen whom Scrooge was careful to impress. Point out the repeated 'a business point of view'. Ask: *What point is the author making?* (Business success or wealth do not make people care about us.) Point out that he keeps looking for himself among the people. Ask: *Why does Scrooge listen to the conversation in the beetling shop with 'detestation and disgust'?* (The items have been stolen from a dead body.) *What makes Scrooge shudder 'from head to foot'?* Ask the children to discuss question 11 on the Guided reading bookmark.

Stave Four, part 2

(from 'He recoiled in terror…' to the end of Stave Four)

Comment on the writer's strong vocabulary ('recoiled in terror') to convey Scrooge's emotion. Ask: *Which words suggest that Scrooge feels compelled to look around the dark room?* ('secret impulse') Read aloud the paragraph beginning 'Oh, cold, cold, rigid, dreadful Death'. Explain that Scrooge thinks he can hear these words when he looks at the dead man. Ask: *What does Scrooge now understand about a miserly person?* (No one cares when he dies.) *Is he relieved when the ghost shows him someone who feels emotion at the man's death?* (No, because the emotion is pleasure.) Consider the changes in the Cratchit family and use question 4 on the Guided reading bookmark for discussion. Point out that Scrooge still does not know the dead man's identity. What does Scrooge ask the ghost to show him? ('what I shall be in days to come.') Ask: *Why does Scrooge tremble when the ghost takes him to a graveyard and points to a grave? What promises does Scrooge finally make?* Discuss the significance of the ghost's hand trembling. Is the ghost indicating that Scrooge has a chance not to end up as this unloved dead man? Ask the children to discuss questions 3 and 8 on the Guided reading bookmark.

Stave Five

Comment on Scrooge's wet face, evidence of his tearful struggle with the spirit. Ask: *Why is Scrooge pleased to find the bed-curtains intact?* (Scrooge thinks that they are proof that the ghost showed him things that *may* be, not what *will* be.) *How must Scrooge change to stop the ghost's predictions coming true?* Identify changes in Scrooge's manner and behaviour: cheerful words; friendly greetings; generosity; humble apologies; pleasure in his family's company; enjoyment of Christmas. Ask: *What is the most rewarding thing he does?* (He prevents the death of Tiny Tim.) Examine the final paragraph. Ask: *Do the spirits visit again?* Point out the author's light-hearted play on words: 'spirits' means ghosts and strong alcoholic drinks; 'abstinence' usually refers to giving up alcohol. Is Dickens addressing the reader in his final two sentences? Ask the children to discuss question 12 on the Guided reading bookmark.

A Christmas Carol
by Charles Dickens

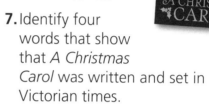

Focus on... Meaning

1. What do you think Charles Dickens wants the reader to feel about Scrooge? Does Dickens want the character to be disliked or pitied? Explain why you say this.

2. What predictions can you make about what may happen in the story from the title and the first paragraphs of this stave?

3. Why is money important in this story? How does it affect Scrooge's behaviour and feelings? What message is the author giving to the reader?

4. Explain why the reader might find Tiny Tim a more important character than Bob Cratchit's other children.

Focus on... Organisation

5. Do you think the author uses dialogue effectively? Give an example and explain how it adds to the story.

6. Why does the author divide the story into long staves? Is it an effective feature?

SCHOLASTIC
READ & RESPOND
Bringing the best books to life in the classroom

A Christmas Carol
by Charles Dickens

Focus on... Language and features

7. Identify four words that show that *A Christmas Carol* was written and set in Victorian times.

8. What devices does the author use in this section to build up atmosphere and information about the characters and the setting?

Focus on... Purpose, viewpoints and effects

9. What point do you think the author is trying to make in this part of the story? Explain why you say this.

10. Do you think Scrooge changes his attitude to his nephew, Fred, during the story? Why? Give examples to support your opinion.

11. Is the author making a serious point here or is he just writing an effective ghost story? Give evidence to support your answer.

12. Which character(s) does the author want you to sympathise with most by the end of the story? Give reasons for your opinion.

SCHOLASTIC
READ & RESPOND
Bringing the best books to life in the classroom

SHARED READING ▶

Extract 1

- In this extract from Stave One, Scrooge talks to a gentleman who has come unexpectedly to his office on Christmas Eve.

- Read aloud the lengthy opening speech. Comment on the gentleman's formal Victorian politeness, circling 'desirable', 'provision' and 'necessaries'. Underline 'usually' and the repeated 'common'. Ask: *What do these words emphasise?* (The poor lack what is normal for others.) Underline 'taking up a pen'. Ask: *What does the gentleman anticipate writing?* (An amount of money next to Scrooge's name.)

- Let the children read out paragraph two, Scrooge's reply. Ask: *How does it contrast with the gentleman's speech in form and meaning?* (It is brief and uncharitable.)

- Underline later references to punishment of the poor: 'prisons', 'union workhouses', 'Treadmill', 'Poor Law'. Ask: *What is the gentleman's attitude to these? What is Scrooge's? Which character's viewpoint does Dickens want the reader to agree with?*

- Investigate the gentleman's lengthy speech in the middle of the extract. Circle 'meat and drink' and 'means of warmth'. What effect does the gentleman expect these words to have? (Scrooge will feel shocked that people lack these.) Circle 'want' and 'keenly'. Can the children supply synonyms?

- Ask: *What does Scrooge mean by replying 'Nothing!' What does the gentleman mistakenly assume?* (That Scrooge wants to donate anonymously.)

- Investigate the extract's final three paragraphs. Ask: *How are the two characters' roles reversed?* (Scrooge becomes the dominant speaker.) *What is Scrooge trying to justify? What is his argument?* (He does not celebrate Christmas, so he should not pay for the poor to make merry.)

Extract 2

- This extract is from Stave Three, when the Cratchit family enjoy their Christmas Day lunch.

- Investigate the long first paragraph. Comment on the short, dramatic opening statement. Circle complimentary nouns linked to the goose: 'tenderness', 'flavour', 'size', 'cheapness' and 'admiration'. Ask: *What impression do these create?* (The family thinks the goose is perfect.) *Which words reveal that it is not very big for such a large family?* Circle 'Eked out' and 'sufficient'.

- Underline 'nervous'. Suggest that Dickens wants the reader to wonder why Mrs Cratchit should be worried about a pudding. Can the children suggest why?

- Point out that paragraph two answers the reader's question about why Mrs Cratchit is 'nervous'. Highlight 'Suppose' at the beginning of three sentences. Ask: *What punctuation mark is noticeable in paragraph two?* Circle the exclamation marks. *Why are they used?* (They emphasise the increasingly imagined disasters as everyone anticipates the Christmas pudding.)

- Ask: *What is the pudding compared to in paragraph three? Which word introduces the comparison?* ('like') *What literary device is Dickens using?* (a simile) Underline 'like a speckled cannon-ball' and circle 'speckled'. Ask: *Why is 'speckled' an appropriate description?* (The pudding is dotted with currants and other dried fruit.)

- Examine the final two sentences. Underline 'flat heresy' and discuss the meaning. (Heresy is an opinion contrary to what is normally accepted.) Ask: *What would it be wrong for a family member to say? What is emphasised about the Cratchits in the final sentence?* (The pudding was too small for their large family. Their gratitude for the little they have.)

Extract 3

- Taken from Stave Five, this is part of the story's climax: a changed Scrooge emerges from his house on Christmas Day to celebrate with others.

- Read aloud the first paragraph. Ask: *What is different about Scrooge's manner?* Underline 'delighted smile' and 'irresistibly pleasant'. *How does Scrooge's new behaviour affect the way other people treat him?* (They wish him 'Merry Christmas'.) Circle 'blithe'. Ask: *What does it mean? Why is this an appropriate adjective in this story?*

- Who comes towards Scrooge in paragraph two? Why does seeing the gentleman send 'a pang across his heart'? (Scrooge is ashamed of what he said to him on Christmas Eve.) Underline 'but he knew what path lay straight before him, and he took it'. Ask: *How does Scrooge show courage here? What is making him behave properly?*

- Examine paragraph five. Ask: *How does Scrooge show humility? Which words are an apology?* Underline 'Allow me to ask your pardon'.

- Direct the children to count the paragraphs from 'My dear sir' to the end of the extract. Ask: *Why has Dickens begun a new paragraph so often?* Remind the children about direct speech rules: a new paragraph is started whenever someone begins or finishes speaking.

- Circle 'farthing'. Ask: *What is it? What is it a further reminder of?* (An old-fashioned coin. The coin reminds the reader that this is a Victorian story.)

- Read the final paragraph aloud. Ask: *Can you complete the final word? Would 'munificence' fit the context?* Discuss the meaning of the word and why it might fit here.

Extract 4

- This extract, from a non-fiction book about strange beliefs, provides information about people's interest in ghosts.

- Highlight the title. Explain that it indicates what the text is about.

- Underline and read aloud the opening statement. What does it achieve? (It introduces and defines the subject.) Read aloud the next two sentences and discuss the first paragraph's function. Point out that the paragraph introduces the topic of ghosts and answers the questions 'What?', 'Who?' and 'How?'

- Question the children about divisions in the remaining text. (paragraphs) Underline the bold words before paragraphs two to five. Explain that such sub headings are common in information texts. What is their purpose? (They help the reader to access information.)

- Circle dates, times and names: 'Charles Dickens', 'Victorians', 'Wilkie Collins', 'Elizabeth Gaskell', 'Christmas', '1642', *'A Christmas Carol'*, *'All the Year Round'*. Emphasise that they identify times and name real people and events, essential in a text giving historical information.

- Circle 'periodical'. Ask: *What is it?* (A magazine published at regular intervals.) The correct term gives authenticity to the text.

- Read paragraph three aloud. Refer to Stave One of the novel and the chains attached to the Ghost of Jacob Marley and the loud bells ringing in the house. Confirm that Dickens' references are typical of Victorian ghost stories.

- Underline 'is denied' in the first paragraph and 'were contributed' in the final paragraph. Identify each as a passive verb: a verb in which the person or thing receiving the action is the subject of the sentence. Circle and identify 'existence' as the subject of the first passive verb; circle and identify 'Ghost stories' as the subject of the second.

 # Extract 1

Stave One

"At this festive season of the year, Mr Scrooge," said the gentleman, taking up a pen, "it is more than usually desirable that we should make some slight provision for the poor and destitute, who suffer greatly at the present time. Many thousands are in want of common necessaries; hundreds of thousands are in want of common comforts, sir."

"Are there no prisons?" asked Scrooge.

"Plenty of prisons," said the gentleman, laying down the pen again.

"And the union workhouses?" demanded Scrooge. "Are they still in operation?"

"They are. Still," returned the gentleman, "I wish I could say they were not."

"The Treadmill and the Poor Law are in full vigour, then?" said Scrooge.

"Both very busy, sir."

"Oh! I was afraid, from what you said at first, that something had occurred to stop them in their useful course," said Scrooge. "I am very glad to hear it."

"Under the impression that they scarcely furnish Christian cheer of mind or body to the multitude," returned the gentleman, "a few of us are endeavouring to raise a fund to buy the poor some meat and drink, and means of warmth. We choose this time, because it is a time, of all others, when want is keenly felt, and abundance rejoices. What shall I put you down for?"

"Nothing!" Scrooge replied.

"You wish to be anonymous?"

"I wish to be left alone," said Scrooge. "Since you ask me what I wish, gentlemen, that is my answer. I don't make merry myself at Christmas, and I can't afford to make idle people merry. I help to support the establishments I have mentioned – they cost enough; and those who are badly off must go there."

"Many can't go there; and many would rather die."

"If they would rather die," said Scrooge, "they had better do it, and decrease the surplus population."

 # Extract 2

Stave Three

There never was such a goose. Bob said he didn't believe there ever was such a goose cooked. Its tenderness and flavour, size and cheapness, were the themes of universal admiration. Eked out by the apple-sauce and mashed potatoes, it was a sufficient dinner for the whole family; indeed, as Mrs Cratchit said with great delight (surveying one small atom of a bone upon the dish), they hadn't ate it all at last! Yet every one had had enough, and the youngest Cratchits, in particular, were steeped in sage and onion to the eyebrows! But now, the plates being changed by Miss Belinda, Mrs Cratchit left the room alone – too nervous to bear witnesses – to take the pudding up, and bring it in.

Suppose it should not be done enough! Suppose it should break in turning out! Suppose somebody should have got over the wall of the back-yard and stolen it, while they were merry with the goose – a supposition at which the two young Cratchits became livid! All sorts of horrors were supposed.

Hallo! A great deal of steam! The pudding was out of the copper. A smell like a washing-day! That was the cloth. A smell like an eating-house and a pastry cook's next door to each other, with a laundress's next door to that! That was the pudding! In half a minute Mrs Cratchit entered – flushed, but smiling proudly – with the pudding, like a speckled cannon-ball, so hard and firm, blazing in half of half-a-quartern of ignited brandy, and bedight with Christmas holly stuck into the top.

Oh, a wonderful pudding! Bob Cratchit said, and calmly too, that he regarded it as the greatest success achieved by Mrs Cratchit since their marriage. Mrs Cratchit said now the weight was off her mind, she would confess she had her doubts about the quantity of flour. Everybody had something to say about it, but nobody said or thought it was at all a small pudding for a large family. It would have been flat heresy to do so. Any Cratchit would have blushed to hint at such a thing.

Extract 3

Stave Five

He dressed himself "all in his best", and at last got out into the streets. The people were by this time pouring forth, as he had seen them with the Ghost of Christmas Present; and walking with his hands behind him, Scrooge regarded everyone with a delighted smile. He looked so irresistibly pleasant, in a word, that three or four good-humoured fellows said, "Good morning, sir! A Merry Christmas to you!" And Scrooge said often afterwards that, of all the blithe sounds he had ever heard, those were the blithest in his ears.

He had not gone far when, coming on towards him, he beheld the portly gentleman who had walked into his counting-house the day before, and said, "Scrooge and Marley's, I believe?" It sent a pang across his heart to think how this old gentleman would look upon him when they met; but he knew what path lay straight before him, and he took it.

"My dear sir," said Scrooge, quickening his pace, and taking the old gentleman by both his hands, "how do you do? I hope you succeeded yesterday. It was very kind of you. A Merry Christmas to you, sir!"

"Mr Scrooge?"

"Yes," said Scrooge. "That is my name, and I fear it may not be pleasant to you. Allow me to ask your pardon. And will you have the goodness ——" Here Scrooge whispered in his ear.

"Lord bless me!" cried the gentleman, as if his breath were gone. "My dear Mr Scrooge, are you serious?"

"If you please," said Scrooge, "Not a farthing less. A great many back-payments are included in it, I assure you. Will you do me that favour?"

"My dear sir," said the other, shaking hands with him, "I don't know what to say to such munifi–"

READ&**RESPOND** A Christmas Carol **17**

 # Extract 4

Ghosts

A ghost is supposed to be the spirit of a dead person. Although some people claim that there are ghosts, their existence is denied by scientists. Many other words are used for 'ghost': spectre, phantom or spirit.

Entertainment

A ghost may be featured in a book, film or play. A strong atmosphere is created and the audience's attention is gained. The audience may be frightened, but in a controlled, safe environment, knowing that they are reading or watching fiction.

The Victorian Age

Stories about ghosts were very popular in Victorian times. Christmas Eve was a traditional time to sit around the fire and tell frightening ghost stories to one another. The stories often involved sudden, unexplained changes between darkness and light and frightening noises, such as clanking chains, creaking floors and doors and moaning voices. Gas lamps and flickering candles were used by the Victorians; these created an eerie atmosphere, where the light and shadows easily tricked people into hallucinations and supposed ghost sightings.

Christmas

Christmas time has long been linked with ghosts. For example, just before Christmas in 1642, shepherds were reported to have seen ghostly soldiers fighting in the sky. The link between ghosts and Christmas was strengthened by Charles Dickens with his story *A Christmas Carol*.

Victorian ghost writers

Dickens had a strong influence on Victorian readers and the popularity of the ghost story genre was increased. In addition to *A Christmas Carol*, other short ghost stories were published by Dickens in his periodical *All the Year Round*. Ghost stories were contributed to this magazine by other important Victorian writers such as Wilkie Collins and Elizabeth Gaskell.

GRAMMAR, PUNCTUATION & SPELLING ▶

1. Marking boundaries

Objective
To use semi-colons, colons or dashes to mark boundaries between independent clauses.

What you need
Copies of *A Christmas Carol*, photocopiable page 22 'Marking boundaries'.

What to do
- After reading Stave One, dictate the following for the children to write on individual whiteboards: 'Scrooge was unpleasant to his nephew he was actually rude.' Let the children hold up their whiteboards. Do most show two sentences? Are there alternatives?

- Write on the whiteboard: 'Scrooge was unpleasant to his nephew – he was actually rude.' and 'Scrooge was unpleasant to his nephew; he was actually rude.' Indicate the use of one sentence. Ask: *Why can this be better than using two sentences?* Identify a dash and a semi-colon, separating independent clauses. Ask: *Which punctuation mark is less formal?* (dash)

- Display this sentence: 'Scrooge recognised the face on the knocker: it was Jacob Marley.' Identify the colon as another means of separation. It introduces more information.

- Give out copies of photocopiable page 22, 'Marking Boundaries'. Explain that the children must decide where and how to divide the sentences into two independent clauses. Afterwards discuss the children's written results. Suggest that 'correct' punctuation often depends on writer preference, so their answers may vary.

Differentiation
Support: Revise the differences between punctuation marks.

Extension: Ask the children to adapt a story they have written, using these punctuation marks.

2. Using suffixes

Objective
To use suffixes to convert nouns or adjectives into verbs.

What you need
Copies of *A Christmas Carol*, teacher-made photocopiable sheet (optional).

What to do
- Introduce the term 'suffix': a group of letters added to the end of a word, turning it into another word. Comment that Scrooge's nephew talks about the 'origin' of Christmas and the customs that 'originate' from it. Write 'originate' on the whiteboard. Divide the verb into two parts: the noun 'origin' and the group of letters 'ate'. Identify 'ate' as a suffix used to form verbs.

- Write these root words on the whiteboard: 'note', 'dark', 'standard', 'legal', 'sharp', 'class'. Display six suffixes: 'en', 'ise', 'ify', 'en', 'ise', 'ify'. Ask the children to attach each suffix to a root word.

- When they have completed the task, write 'notify' on the whiteboard. Ask: *Did you spot that there was a spelling difficulty?* Explain that some root words change their spelling when a suffix is added ('note' loses 'e' before adding 'ify' to become 'notify'.)

- Create a worksheet of 22 boxes, each containing a root word or suffix: 'simple', 'elastic', 'glory', 'soft', 'deaf', 'pollen', 'apology', 'length', 'real', 'pure', 'false'; 'en', 'en', 'ate', 'ify', 'ise', 'ify', 'en', 'ate', 'ify', 'ise', 'ify'. The children pair the boxes to make verbs. Share answers.

Differentiation
Support: Let children work in pairs.

Extension: Ask the children to create verbs from: 'red', 'slack', 'mobile', 'bright', 'author', 'assassin', 'fright', 'captive', 'equal', 'sad', 'intense'. Which suffixes are used?

3. Passive verbs

Objective
To use passive verbs to affect the presentation of information in a sentence.

What you need
Copies of *A Christmas Carol*, individual copies of Extract 4 on page 18.

What to do
- Complete this activity after reading Stave Two.

- Write this sentence on the whiteboard: 'The clergyman signed the register of Marley's burial'. Ask: *Which word is the verb?* ('signed') *Which subject word does the action?* ('clergyman') Identify 'signed' as an active verb.

- Direct the children to the third sentence of Stave One. Ask: *Which two words form the verb?* ('was signed') Point out that the subject, 'The register', has the action of the verb done to it. Hence, the verb is passive.

- Explain that passive verbs are often used in non-fiction texts. They create an impersonal tone. Display Extract 4 and remind the children of its context. Underline 'is denied' in the first paragraph and 'were contributed' in the final paragraph. Identify each as a passive verb: a verb in which the person or thing receiving the action is the subject of the sentence. Circle and identify 'existence' as the subject of the first passive verb; circle and identify 'Ghost stories' as the subject of the second.

- Give out individual copies of Extract 4. Ask the children to identify six to ten passive verbs and the subject of each verb.

Differentiation
Support: Let the children work in pairs; reduce the number of verbs they identify.

Extension: Ask the children to identify six passive verbs in a class science text book.

4. Using commas

Objective
To use commas to clarify meaning or avoid ambiguity in writing.

What you need
Copies of *A Christmas Carol*.

What to do
- Direct the children to the first three paragraphs of Stave Four. Ask: *Which punctuation mark is used frequently?* (a comma)

- Revise the main uses of commas:
1. Separating items in a list – but not usually before 'and'.
2. Marking off extra information, the commas often in pairs.
3. Following a subordinate clause that begins a sentence, or following a fronted adverbial.

- Explain that commas are also used to avoid writing being ambiguous (having more than one possible meaning). Write this sentence on the board: 'Scrooge listened again thinking that the explanation might lie here'. Discuss its meaning, before adding a comma after 'again'. Explain that without the comma, the reader could think that Scrooge was thinking the same thing again, rather than listening again. Look together for other examples in the book.

- Consider Lynne Truss' ambiguous statement 'the panda eats, shoots and leaves'. Demonstrate how the position of a comma affects its meaning.

- Write this sentence on the board for pairs of children to discuss its two possible meanings: 'If we are going to the cinema then Jack will not be able to come.' ('then' either links to the time of going to the cinema or to Jack). Ask them to write the sentence twice, with a comma in a different place. Let individuals explain the different meanings to the class.

Differentiation
Support: Help children to discuss the different meanings.

Extension: Encourage children to write their own sentences about Christmas Eve, including a comma that makes the meaning clear.

5. Silent letters

Objective
To spell some words with 'silent' letters.

What you need
Copies of *A Christmas Carol*, photocopiable page 23 'Silent letters'.

What to do

- Read aloud this extract from the final pages of the book as the children follow: 'He went to church, and walked about the streets'. Repeat the word 'walked'. Which letter do the children see but not hear? ('l' is silent.) Share other words containing a silent 'l' ('calf', 'balm', 'chalk').

- Read aloud the final paragraph of the book. Draw attention to 'knowledge'. Ask: *Which letter is silent?* ('k')

- List these words on the whiteboard: 'column', 'island', 'knuckle', 'half', 'doubt', 'gnome'. Suggest that the children work in pairs, reading the words to each other and identifying the silent letters.

- Work through the list together, choosing different pairs to circle the silent letter. Offer the answer for class discussion. Does the class agree with the suggested answer?

- Put the children into pairs again, each with their own copy of photocopiable page 23 'Silent letters'. Ask the partners to take turns reading the story to each other. The listener must be on the alert for letters they cannot hear and underline those words on their text. Ask them to circle the silent letters (si**g**ht, **g**hostly, **k**nees, **k**nocking, pa**l**ms, mois**t**ened, **w**retched, gli**s**tening, moon**l**ight, **w**reck, dou**b**ted, **w**rinkled, **w**rapped, ti**g**htly, num**b**).

Differentiation
Support: Underline the words on the photocopiable page and ask students to circle the silent letters.

Extension: Children write a new story containing six words with silent letters and read it to a partner. Can the partner identify the silent letters?

6. Spelling homophones

Objective
To continue to distinguish between homophones and other words which are often confused.

What you need
Copies of *A Christmas Carol*, dictionaries, photocopiable page 24 'Spelling homophones'.

What to do

- Write on the whiteboard: 'The clanging <u>ascent</u> of Marley's Ghost was terrifying'. Can partners tell each other the underlined word's meaning? Confirm 'coming up'.

- Add to the whiteboard: 'The Spirit did not wait for Scrooge's <u>assent</u>.' Ask partners to share the underlined word's meaning. Confirm 'agreement'. When the sentences are read aloud, what do the children notice about the underlined words? (They sound the same.)

- Identify 'ascent' and 'assent' as homophones: words pronounced in the same way, but with a different meaning. Share other homophones. Use 'steal'/'steel', 'heard'/'herd', 'new'/'knew', and 'who's'/'whose' in oral sentences for the children to identify, define and spell.

- Write these words separately and in a random order on the whiteboard: 'serial'/'cereal', 'isle'/'aisle', 'aloud'/'allowed', 'bridle'/'bridal', 'draught'/'draft', 'dissent'/'descent'. Explain that the words must be matched in pairs of homophones. Let partners work together, using dictionaries to check meanings. Bring the class back together to discuss the pairs of words and the different meanings of the words in each pair.

- Give out copies of photocopiable page 24 'Spelling homophones'. Encourage the children to check meanings of both words in a pair before choosing the correct one to write in each space.

Differentiation
Support: Read aloud to children, explaining the pairs of words before they write.

Extension: Ask children to think of 8–10 more pairs of homophones and to use each of them correctly in a written sentence.

Marking boundaries

● Write each sentence, adding a dash (–), semi-colon (;) or colon (:) so that two independent clauses are separated.

1. Ebenezer Scrooge was not generous in fact, he was miserly!

_____

_____

2. He had one word to describe Christmas jollity it was 'humbug'.

_____

_____

3. Scrooge gave his clerk a paid holiday it was one day a year.

_____

_____

4. That day was special it was Christmas Day.

_____

5. The clerk had a fire it was too small for warmth.

_____

6. The poor man tried to keep warm he put on a scarf!

_____

7. Scrooge was not an imaginative man he did not fear strange noises.

_____

_____

8. Now he remembered what he had heard about ghosts in haunted houses they dragged chains.

_____

_____

Silent letters

● Listen as your partner reads this story aloud. Underline fifteen words that have a silent letter and circle the silent letter.

He was terrified at the sight of the ghostly figure in front of him; his knees were knocking and his palms moistened.

The wretched creature was glistening in the moonlight in front of him. It's fair to say that he felt a wreck, he wanted to run but doubted his legs would allow him to escape. He closed his eyes, wrinkled his nose and wrapped his coat tightly around himself. The old man was numb with fear.

Spelling homophones

● Complete Bob Cratchit's diary entry. For each space, choose the correct word from each pair/set of homophones.

I was very pleased to be _____ the day off today. I had thought that old Scrooge _____ make me work this year, I couldn't _____ the thought of that.

As ever on Christmas _____ , I took Tiny Tim to church with me. Despite the _____ in the old building the boy sat there good as gold; never before have I _____ such sweet singing as I did from him today.

Mrs Cratchit worked so hard and _____ a feast fit for a king. The goose was a _____ to behold, all we could do was _____ in wonder. The pudding was also _____ ; the children loved it when we set it alight and _____ faces were a picture! When we had eaten there was not a scrap left, no _____ .

I am so grateful on this happy day for the love and support of my wonderful family. I am blessed to be a _____ and a husband. We may not have _____ pennies to rub together, but we are rich in so many ways.

maid / made	stair / stare	too / two / to
grate / great	bare / bear	allowed / aloud
they're / their / there	waste / waist	site / sight
wood / would	morning / mourning	draft / draught
herd / heard	father / farther	

PLOT, CHARACTER & SETTING ▶

1. Story journal

Objective
To summarise the main ideas drawn from more than one paragraph, identifying key details that support the main ideas.

What you need
Copies of *A Christmas Carol*, photocopiable page 29 'Story journal'.

Cross curricular link
Art and design

What to do

- After reading the first half of Stave One, suggest using a journal to keep track of the plot and maintain interest. Hold partner, then class, discussions about information to include (for example, events since the last journal entry; character development; points of interest; setting; unusual language; personal response; predictions). Propose making entries after every 12 pages or so.

- Display the headings from photocopiable page 29 'Story Journal', adapting the first two to 'What has happened so far?' and 'Characters'. Organise paired, then class, discussions relating the first half of Stave One to each heading. Encourage personal reactions to the book.

- For the final section, talk about varied media forms. The children may express their response to the chapter with an illustration or poster, or may use a well-known painting or piece of music.

- Give everyone photocopiable page 29 'Story journal' and an exercise book. Suggest using the sheet as a template for future entries.

Differentiation
Support: Let partners work together, but encourage a personal reaction to the story.

Extension: Encourage longer entries and wider variation and research for supporting art forms.

2. Finding answers

Objective
To predict what might happen from details stated and implied.

What you need
Copies of *A Christmas Carol*, photocopiable page 30 'Finding answers'.

What to do

- After reading Stave One, help the children to scan the text again. Draw attention to the characters we meet in this first section of the book. Ask: *Which character's name do you most notice? Does a dead man seem to have a surprising amount of attention paid to him? Who do you think will be important in the rest of the book? Which subject will matter?* Encourage the children to talk in pairs before discussing as a class.

- Give out photocopiable page 30 'Finding answers'. Ask the children to fill in the 'What I know about' section, summarising what they know so far about Scrooge, Jacob Marley and Scrooge's attitude to Christmas.

- Ask: *Are some questions unanswered?* (For example, will seeing Jacob Marley affect Scrooge's attitude to Christmas?) Ask the children to summarise missing information in the 'What I don't know about yet' section.

- Invite the children to think about how the story will end. Direct them to the box at the bottom of the photocopiable sheet to write their prediction.

Differentiation
Support: Use partner discussion as a preparation for writing. Draw children's attention to specific points to focus on.

Extension: Widen the study to include Scrooge's nephew and his clerk. Suggest the children check their prediction at different points in the story, amending as the story progresses.

3. Pictures in words

Objective
To discuss and evaluate how authors use language, considering the impact on the reader.

What you need
Copies of *A Christmas Carol*.

What to do
- After reading Stave One, suggest that the meeting between Marley's Ghost and Scrooge is one of the most dramatic incidents so far in the book. With no illustration, the writer relies on effective language.

- Propose dividing an investigation of this incident into four sections. Ask the children to fold a piece of paper into four storyboard squares with these headings: 1. What Marley's Ghost looks like; 2. The noises Scrooge hears; 3. What the ghost shows and tells Scrooge; 4. How Scrooge is left feeling.

- Begin reading at 'After several turns he sat down again' in Stave One and read about two pages. Using partner and class discussion, ask: *What is revealed about Marley's Ghost? What physical details are given?* (his clothes and pigtail) *Which language is effective?* ('death-cold eyes'; 'transparent'). Ask the children to record in square 1 how the reader feels about the ghost's appearance and which language helps.

- Advise partners to read, discuss and examine about two pages at a time before writing independently in the storyboard squares. Revise personification, similes and onomatopoeia. Remind them to explain the information given, to think about how the reader is affected and to quote effective language.

Differentiation
Support: Encourage greater partner collaboration and accept less writing.

Extension: Ask children to investigate in the same way when Scrooge first arrives home and sees Marley's face on the knocker.

4. Checking meanings

Objective
To check that the book makes sense to them, exploring the meaning of words in context.

What you need
Copies of *A Christmas Carol*, dictionaries.

Cross curricular link
History

What to do
- Use this activity after reading Stave One. Remind the children that this book was written in 1843, during the reign of Queen Victoria. Explain that Victoria had a long reign at a time of rapid changes and developments: railways, leisure activities, hospitals, new medicines, greater prosperity. Point out that the vocabulary in the book often reflects Victorian times and the fact that it was a story written for adults.

- Write these words on the whiteboard: 'counting-house', 'workhouse', 'liberality', 'credentials', 'comforter', 'half a crown', 'shilling', 'brazier', melancholy'. Explain that they have all been used in the first part of Stave One.

- Ask the children to copy the list of words, before working with a partner to locate them in the text and to discuss their likely meanings. Are the words in the dictionary? Ask them to write a brief definition or explanation for each.

- Repeat the exercise with these words from the second part of Stave One: 'ledger', 'penance', 'lamentation', 'cellar', 'cravat', 'tassels', 'transparent', 'phenomenon'. Again let the children find the words in the text and write definitions from the dictionary before you share the meanings.

Differentiation
Support: Give adult support locating the words in the book. Give access to an alphabet line when using a dictionary.

Extension: Ask the children to list another six words in Stave One whose meanings they are unsure of. Encourage them to define each in a single word or short phrase.

5. Following structures

Objective
To read books that are structured in different ways.

What you need
Copies of *A Christmas Carol*.

Cross curricular link
History

What to do
- Complete this activity after finishing the book.

- Consider the writer's organisation of *A Christmas Carol*. Ask: *How is it divided?* (staves) *Do you have other suggestions for its structure?* Suggest that there could be shorter chapters, sections or settings, with headings to correspond to where or when events take place.

- Suggest that time is important to this book's plot and structure. Remind the children of the opening paragraph and its emphasis on the past: Marley's burial. Ask: *Which spirits later lead Scrooge through events?* Discuss the order in which Scrooge is shown events. Ask: *Is Dickens right to describe Scrooge's present day behaviour before we learn about his sad boyhood?*

- Ask: *At which time of the year do the present-day events occur?* (Christmas) Point out that most of the story takes place on Christmas Eve and Christmas morning. Ask: *Why does Scrooge become confused about time? Why, on Christmas morning, does he have to ask a boy what day it is?* (In one night, Scrooge has been taken into the past and into the future.)

- Ask children to write two paragraphs about how Dickens helps the reader to follow the story and to understand which events are in the past, present or future. How would the children have presented the story differently?

Differentiation
Support: Expect less writing and support the children with sentence openers.

Extension: Ask the children to name six important events in the story for a partner to sequence.

6. Considering others

Objective
To identify and discuss themes and conventions in a wide range of writing.

What you need
Copies of *A Christmas Carol*.

Cross curricular link
History

What to do
- Do this activity after finishing the book.

- Suggest that the treatment of people in need is a strong theme in this book. Investigate the opposing attitudes of Scrooge and the gentleman who is collecting donations, by scanning their dialogue in Stave One. Ask: *How do their attitudes differ? Which character do you think Dickens sympathises with?* Ask the children to write a paragraph about Scrooge's attitude towards people in need and how he thinks their needs should be managed.

- Direct the children to the scene with the carol singer halfway through Stave One, and Scrooge's departure from his office. Ask: *What is uncharitable in his treatment of the carol singer and his clerk?* Comment on the clerk's small fire and Scrooge's grumbling about celebrating Christmas Day. Ask the children to write a paragraph about Scrooge's treatment of others and what it shows about him.

- Direct the children to Scrooge and the gentleman's dialogue in Stave Five. Ask: *Has Scrooge changed his views since Christmas Eve? What does Scrooge think about the treatment of the poor now? How does he prove that he has changed?* Ask the children to write a paragraph about how Scrooge changes his attitudes to others, particularly to those poorer than he is.

Differentiation
Support: Encourage partner discussions before writing. Offer help with textual references.

Extension: Expect more writing and greater understanding of the text.

PLOT, CHARACTER & SETTING

7. Asking questions

Objective
To ask questions to improve their understanding of the text.

What you need
Copies of *A Christmas Carol*.

What to do

- Do this activity after finishing the book.

- Ask the children to write the headings 'Stave One, part 1', 'Stave One, part 2', 'Stave Two, part 1', 'Stave Two, part 2'.

- Guide the children through scanning Stave One, part 1. (See the text divisions in 'Guided reading' on page 9.) Ask: *What questions are in your mind by the end of this section?* Encourage partner discussion and share some ideas. Write one example question on the whiteboard: *Will something terrible happen in the fog?* Ask the children to write down their own two questions.

- Scan Stave One, part 2 together. Encourage partner discussion about questions they want answered by the end of the Stave. Ask the children to write down two questions. Repeat the scanning, thinking, talking and writing process for both parts of Stave Two.

- Suggest that by the end of the book, most questions should have been answered. Ask the children to write the answers, with book quotations or references. Are any questions left unanswered?

- Let the children consider the whole book and unanswered questions provoked earlier, for example, *Could Scrooge be dreaming?* Ask the children to write down two or three questions they still have. Ask: *How could these be answered now?* (in a sequel)

Differentiation
Support: Accept one question at each stage. Offer guidance with finding answers.

Extension: Expect more questions and specific location of answers.

8. Understanding characters

Objective
To infer characters' feelings, thoughts and motives from their actions.

What you need
Copies of *A Christmas Carol*, photocopiable page 31, 'Understanding characters'.

Cross curricular link
PSHE

What to do

- Complete this activity after finishing the book.

- Ask: *Who is the main character?* (Scrooge) Point out that the book moves between the present and the past. Ask: *Does Scrooge change?* Discuss the different pictures presented of the main character.

- Let partners discuss how writers can reveal a character's personality (through actions, dialogue, comments by other characters). Make a class list.

- Point out that Dickens often allows readers to form their own opinion, rather than telling them what to think. Refer the children to the scene in Stave One when Scrooge and his clerk discuss Christmas Day. The reader may infer that Scrooge is mean-spirited when he grumbles about the clerk having the whole of Christmas Day off. From the clerk's comment 'If quite convenient, sir' the reader infers humility and acceptance of such poor treatment.

- Give out copies of photocopiable page 31, 'Understanding characters'. Suggest that the children concentrate on one stage of Scrooge's life at a time, working with a partner and searching the text for the actions and words that allow the reader to infer characteristics. Encourage the children to make their own adjective selection. Finally, ask them to write four new adjectives, one for each stage of Scrooge's life.

Differentiation
Support: Reduce the choice of adjectives, leaving only the most appropriate.

Extension: Ask the children to use the chosen adjectives in a full sketch of one of the Scrooges.

Story journal

● Use the headings to help you remember what you have recently read in the book.

Date:

Part reached

My reaction to the story so far

What I think will happen next

What has happened since the last entry?

My idea for a supporting art form for this section

Setting references

Special vocabulary and points of interest

Character developments

Atmosphere and attitudes

Rate the story:

Finding answers

- Fill in what you know and what you still have to find out.
- Then write what you think may happen in the future.

	What I know about...	What I don't know about yet...
Scrooge 		
Jacob Marley 		
Scrooge's attitude to Christmas		

What I predict will happen by the end of the story...

Understanding characters

- Draw lines to join two appropriate adjectives to Scrooge at each stage of his life.
- Then write four adjectives of your own and join them.

high-spirited

selfish

hard-hearted

solitary

anti-social

melancholy

charitable

homesick

lonely

rude

sad

polite

caring

generous

greedy

friendly

humble

miserable

bullying

happy

loving

hospitable

grateful

1. _____   3. _____

2. _____   4. _____

TALK ABOUT IT ▶

1. Ignore or invite?

Objective
To participate in discussions and debates.

What you need
Copies of *A Christmas Carol*, photocopiable page 35 'Ignore or invite?'

Cross curricular link
Citizenship

What to do
- After reading Stave One, direct the children to Fred's visit to Scrooge, his Christmas greetings and his dinner invitation. Ask the children to consider whether Fred should have bothered inviting him.

- Put the children into pairs with a copy of photocopiable page 35 'Ignore or invite?' Encourage partner and class discussion of the statements on the sheet. Point out that some statements may support either case (for example, Scrooge plans to be on his own).

- Ask partners to discuss and decide which side to support: Fred going home or inviting Scrooge. (Ensure there are children supporting both sides.) The children must cut out and then choose the statements they think will support that case.

- Invite suggestions for other reasons to ignore or invite Scrooge. Take the role of chairing the debate and listening to arguments from both sides. Allow everyone to speak. Finally, sum up what you have heard. Allow a 'free' vote, in which they vote as individuals, not as part of a group.

Differentiation
Support: Suggest children read out the statement that they think is the most effective argument.

Extension: Ask children to argue a third way: making a surprise visit to Scrooge's house on Christmas Day.

2. Frozen moments

Objective
To use spoken language to develop understanding through speculating, hypothesising, imagining and exploring ideas.

What you need
Copies of *A Christmas Carol*, photocopiable page 36 'Frozen moments'.

Cross curricular link
Drama

What to do
- After reading Stave Two, explain the term 'freeze-frame': the children take on the roles of story characters and create a still picture of a moment in the story.

- Arrange the children into groups of four. Give each group a card from photocopiable page 36 'Frozen moments'. Ask them to scan their part of the story to see what the characters are doing and feeling. The group then creates a freeze-frame of the scene. Allow 10–15 minutes for scanning, group discussion and rehearsal.

- Let each group present their freeze-frame to the class. Can the class identify the story moment and characters? Select individuals to step out of the tableau and say what they are thinking. For other characters in the tableau, encourage the audience to consider what they seem to be thinking.

- Talk about the relevance of facial expression and body language in freeze-frames. Ask the class: *Which expressions and body language helped you understand what they were thinking?*

Differentiation
Support: Offer suggestions for poses.

Extension: Ask the children to plan alternative freeze-frames that will suggest different character feelings.

3. In the hot seat

Objective
To take part in role play; to infer characters' feelings, thoughts and motives.

What you need
Copies of *A Christmas Carol*, a night cap or other Scrooge-related prop (optional).

Cross curricular link
PSHE

What to do

- Use this activity after reading Stave Three.

- Suggest that the reader sometimes wants more detail about characters' feelings and motives than is given explicitly in the text. For example *How does Martha feel about her job as an apprentice? Why is Scrooge eager to watch Fred's party for longer? Why does Fred laugh so much?*

- Focus on Scrooge and what he has been shown by the Second Spirit. Ask the children, after partner discussion, to agree on and write two questions they would like to ask Scrooge. Organise the children into groups of four to compare questions. Ask them to agree on two group questions.

- Explain the term 'hot-seat' (role play in which a character is interviewed). Put yourself in the hot-seat as Scrooge. Turn away and try to make a change to your appearance (add a night cap, for example). Turn and face the class, and invite the groups to ask you their questions, making sure that you answer in role.

- Let groups discuss what they found out about Scrooge's feelings and changing personality. Compare findings as a class.

- Select a different character: Bob Cratchit, Mrs Cratchit, the Second Spirit or Scrooge's nephew, Fred. Repeat the task as a group activity, one group member taking the hot-seat to answer the others' questions.

Differentiation
Support: Provide the children with question starters.

Extension: Ask the children to make close references to the text.

4. What a story!

Objective
To give well-structured narratives for different purposes, including for expressing feelings.

What you need
Copies of *A Christmas Carol*, photocopiable page 37 'What a story!'

Cross curricular link
Drama

What to do

- Complete this activity after reading Stave Three.

- Direct the children to the description of the Cratchit family's Christmas celebration. Point out that although the family is poor, each member has enjoyed a special day. Suggest that they will all be thinking about the day and have a story to tell. Explain that the children are going to tell the story from one character's point of view.

- Guide the children through the main events. Point out Bob's low pay; the efforts made with clothes; the delight in having Martha for the day; the care of the weakest family member, Tiny Tim; the fuss over the goose; the gratitude for very little; the attention given to the pudding; the toast to Scrooge.

- Ask the children to decide which character to be: Mrs Cratchit, Martha, Bob or Peter.

- Give the children photocopiable page 37 'What a story!' and ask them to make notes and sketches to remind them what happened. Emphasise that they will be telling, not reading, their story.

- Let the children practise their storytelling on partners. Organise storytelling groups, so everyone experiences speaking to a group.

Differentiation
Support: Suggest doing pictorial and just one-word notes for a reduced number of cue cards.

Extension: Ask the children to take the role of the watching Scrooge, later telling the story of what he has seen.

▼ TALK ABOUT IT

5. Conscience alley

Objective
To use spoken language to develop understanding through speculating, hypothesising, imagining and exploring ideas.

What you need
Copies of *A Christmas Carol*.

Cross curricular link
PSHE

What to do
- Complete this activity after finishing the book.

- Point out, in Stave Two, Scrooge's desire to change his earlier behaviour to a carol singer and his clerk. Scan these episodes in Stave One and confirm Scrooge's unkind, miserly ways. Suggest that the reader learns eventually that Scrooge is a mixture of good and bad.

- Divide the class into two groups: Group A represents Scrooge's good side, Group B his bad side. Ask Group A to think of comments to persuade Scrooge to give money to the carol singer. Ask Group B to think of comments to encourage him to chase the boy away.

- Organise the two groups into parallel lines facing each other. Take the role of Scrooge and walk down the 'alley' between the lines. As you reach children, nod to them to speak their comments. At the end of the alley, having listened to their voices, make your decision.

- Choose children to act as Scrooge and repeat the conscience alley. Does each Scrooge reach the same decision?

- Try the activity with other situations, for example, when Scrooge speaks to his clerk about having Christmas Day off or when Bob puts on his comforter to keep warm.

Differentiation
Support: Provide sample comments and let children speak with a partner in the conscience alley activity.

Extension: Ask children to plan a conscience alley situation for Martha or Peter Cratchit.

6. Making decisions

Objective
To participate in role play; to develop understanding through speculating, hypothesising, imagining and exploring ideas.

What you need
Copies of *A Christmas Carol*.

What to do
- After completing the book, suggest that minor plot decisions may have a large impact.

- Revisit Fred and Scrooge's encounter in Stave One. Put the children into pairs, with one acting as Fred and one as Scrooge. Pose the hypothetical question: *What if Scrooge accepts the invitation to Christmas dinner?* (Scrooge may become more caring.) On your signal, let partners improvise dialogue for one to two minutes.

- Stop the improvisations, but leave one pair in character for others to question about their feelings and decisions.

- Invite the pairs to repeat the exercise with the gentleman and Scrooge's conversation in Stave One, partners exchanging the role of Scrooge. Pose the hypothetical question: *What if Scrooge agrees, reluctantly, to give a small donation to the poor?* (The ghost of Jacob Marley may not feel the need to appear in the night.) Hot-seat a new pair for the children to question.

- Finally, improvise the scene with Bob Cratchit in Stave Five, asking: *What if Scrooge keeps Bob's salary at the same low level?* (Some of the unhappy future shown by the ghost may come true.)

- As a class, discuss and review their work. What decisions are made? Is Scrooge's fate changed?

Differentiation
Support: Provide children with useful conversation openers.

Extension: Encourage children to pose questions for meetings between Scrooge and the girl with whom he had a contract in Stave Two.

Ignore or invite?

- Cut out all the statements.
- Do you want Fred to invite Scrooge for a Christmas meal or just to ignore him? Choose the statements which support your case.

Scrooge does not want to celebrate Christmas.

Scrooge does not understand love.

Christmas is a time for sharing.

Scrooge plans to be on his own.

Fred is Scrooge's nephew.

Christmas is a time to be among family and friends.

Frozen moments

- Read your part of the story with your group.
- Create a freeze-frame of the scene.

Two pleasant gentleman stand in Scrooge's office in Stave One. They are collecting money to help the poor and homeless. Scrooge is shaking his head uncharitably, refusing their request. Bob, his clerk, shivers as he works in a dim, little area copying letters.

Fred has come to wish his uncle Merry Christmas in Stave One. Fred is cheerful, but Scrooge lacks any Christmas spirit. Bob Cratchit, the clerk, is applauding: he has heard Fred telling Scrooge that Christmas is a time to celebrate.

Scrooge, sitting in his office, is reaching angrily for a ruler in Stave One. A boy on the street is bending down outside at Scrooge's keyhole, singing carols. Bob Cratchit works on his writing. Someone walks by outside, smiling at the sight of a Christmas carol singer.

Scrooge and the First Spirit watch a little boy alone in a room in Stave Two. The boy Scrooge looks sad. A girl, his sister, is about to come into the room. The boy Scrooge has not seen his sister yet.

A jolly Mr and Mrs Fezziwig dance energetically in Stave Two. A fiddler plays, and the young clerk, Scrooge, cheerfully eats and drinks. Everyone is enjoying the party.

Belle sits as two of her children rush to greet their happy father in Stave Two. The father is laden with Christmas toys and presents. The children are rushing to take the presents. Everyone looks happy.

What a story!

● Write notes to complete the cards and use them to help you tell the story from Mrs Cratchit, Martha, Bob or Peter's point of view.

Introducing yourself
Who are you?
How were you feeling this morning?

_____
_____
_____

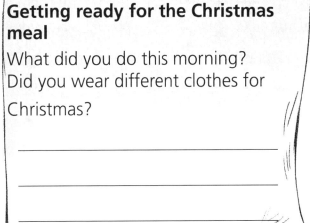

Getting ready for the Christmas meal
What did you do this morning?
Did you wear different clothes for Christmas?

_____
_____

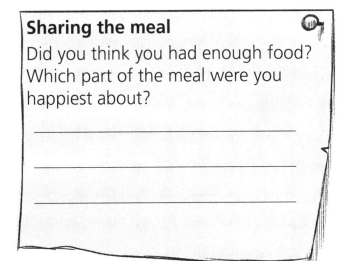

Sharing the meal
Did you think you had enough food?
Which part of the meal were you happiest about?

_____
_____
_____

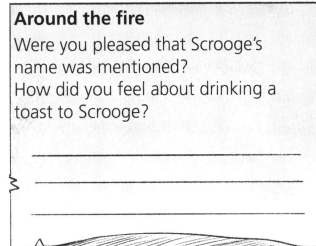

Around the fire
Were you pleased that Scrooge's name was mentioned?
How did you feel about drinking a toast to Scrooge?

_____
_____
_____

Tonight
What are you thinking and feeling now?

_____
_____
_____

GET WRITING ▶

1. Heartless talk

Objective
To identify the audience for and purpose of the writing, selecting the appropriate form and using other similar writing as models for their own.

What you need
Copies of *A Christmas Carol*.

What to do
- Do this activity after reading the first half of Stave One. During the activity encourage paired exchanges before whole-class discussion.

- Comment that Scrooge has a number of interesting conversations in the book. Direct the children to the one with his nephew. Read the dialogue aloud. Ask: *What do you notice about Scrooge's language?* Pick out short, sharp exclamations ('He should!'); extreme comments ('…should be boiled with his own pudding, and buried with a stake of holly through his heart'); word repetition ('Bah!', 'Humbug!').

- Investigate Scrooge's conversation with the gentleman. Point out: Scrooge's extreme views; opposition to mercy; pleasure in the suffering of the poor. Direct the children to Scrooge's words to his clerk. Ask: *Does Scrooge's talk follow the same pattern as before?* Identify examples.

- Ask the children to write a conversation between Scrooge and a new character, for example, someone selling something in the street. After writing their draft conversations alone, the children could read them aloud to each other for reaction and suggestions for improvement.

Differentiation
Support: Let partners collaborate on their writing.

Extension: Suggest children extend their conversations, or write one where Scrooge is involved with a different character.

2. Providing facts

Objective
To write non-narrative material, using further organisational and presentational devices to structure text and to guide the reader.

What you need
Copies of *A Christmas Carol*, Extract 2, Extract 4, photocopiable page 41 'Notes'.

Cross curricular link
History

What to do
- After reading Stave Three, display and read aloud copies of Extracts 2 and 4. In pairs, ask children to talk about why one text is fiction, and one is non-fiction. Share answers. Agree that Extract 2 is fiction because of the made-up characters and events; Extract 4 is non-fiction as it informs the reader of facts.

- Suggest that readers of non-fiction texts often search for specific information; they may not want to read from start to finish. Explain that organisational and presentational devices can act as signposts. Use a non-fiction book to show examples of organisational and presentational devices: headings; subheadings; bullet points; numbers; diagrams; columns; underlining; glossaries; tables.

- Give out individual copies of photocopiable page 41 'Notes'. Ask the children to use the notes to write two paragraphs about Christmas in Victorian times. Remind them that they can re-order the information and group together ideas that cover the same topic. What devices will they use?

Differentiation
Support: Help children to select information for one paragraph.

Extension: Ask the children to write a third paragraph and subheading from the notes.

3. Book review

Objective
To assess the effectiveness of their own and others' writing.

What you need
Copies of *A Christmas Carol*.

What to do
- Complete this activity after finishing the book.

- Ask the children to explain to a partner what a book review is. Share ideas and ask: *What are reviews for? Who writes them? Where are they published? Who reads them?*

- Show the children example book reviews, such as those on the Scholastic website of teacher resources (www.scholastic.co.uk). Explain that there is no set format for a book review. Investigate some common features: book title, author and, if appropriate, illustrator; story information (without revealing too much of the plot); personal opinion on the book; a comment about its suitability for others.

- Hold a class discussion in which the children express their opinions of *A Christmas Carol*. Emphasise that their views are not right or wrong; tastes are personal. However, encourage them to support their views with references to the book. Ask: *What did you particularly enjoy about the book? Where did you think it was most and least successful?*

- Invite the children to write a review of *A Christmas Carol*. Suggest they write a rough draft before producing a polished version.

Differentiation
Support: Offer suggestions and encourage partner discussion when children are deciding what they most liked or disliked, and the reader it would suit.

Extension: Let children write a review of a book they have read recently.

4. Creating an ending

Objective
To plan their writing by identifying the purpose of the writing.

What you need
Copies of *A Christmas Carol*, photocopiable page 42 'Creating an ending'.

What to do
- Complete this activity after finishing the book. Help the children to scan the final chapter. Point out that these pages form the story's ending. Ask: *What is the function of a story's ending?* (Loose ends should be tied up; plot questions may be answered; plot problems ought to be resolved.) Discuss the children's ideas.

- Identify some of these features in *A Christmas Carol*'s ending. Point out that the progress of Scrooge has been followed; his ambition to avoid the future shown to him has been fulfilled; the problem of the Cratchit family's poverty and the survival of Tiny Tim have been solved; questions about Scrooge's future attitude to Christmas have been answered.

- Suggest that the author could have chosen to end the story differently. Let partners tell each other one possible alternative before you share some ideas as a class.

- Ask the children to write a new final stave. Give out individual copies of photocopiable page 42 'Creating an ending' for them to make planning notes. Let partners discuss their completed plans before, independently, writing their own ending.

Differentiation
Support: Suggest the children create picture storyboards of their ending before writing the text.

Extension: Ask the children to plan and talk about a second alternative ending.

▼ GET WRITING

5. Story planning

> **Objective**
> To note and develop initial ideas.
>
> **What you need**
> Copies of *A Christmas Carol*, photocopiable page 43 'Story planning'.
>
> **Cross curricular link**
> History

What to do

- Complete this activity after finishing the book.

- Invite the class to imagine that, after the popularity of this book, the author is to write a sequel the following Christmas in keeping with the original story. Ask: *What could stay the same?* (perhaps the main character, Scrooge; other characters, such as Bob; happy relatives; a Christmas theme; the writing style; Victorian references) *What could change?* (There could be new characters, a new plot, setting, worry or problem.)

- Ask partners to share ideas for a sequel. Prompt them with questions: Ask: *Where is the story set?* (for example, the City of London) *What is the problem?* (Years in the future Scrooge's nephew, Fred, has become miserly.) *How is Fred made aware of this?* (a visit from the ghost of his dead uncle, Scrooge) *What is he warned about?* (future events) *What terrors are there? Are there struggles?* (Fred sees himself in terrible circumstances) *What is the ending?*

- Recap a story's structure of chronological sections: opening; incidents; complications; events to sort them out; ending. Talk about the value of subplots to keep readers interested.

- Give out photocopiable page 43 'Story planning'. Invite the children to complete their plan with brief notes. Keep the plans for the next activity.

> **Differentiation**
> **Support:** Let partners work together on the same story. Provide ideas for one or two sections.
>
> ---
>
> **Extension:** Encourage children to write detailed character notes.

6. Becoming authors

> **Objective**
> To describe settings, characters and atmosphere and integrating dialogue.
>
> **What you need**
> Copies of *A Christmas Carol*, the children's completed story planners from 'Story planning'.
>
> **Cross curricular link**
> History

What to do

- Remind the children of the previous activity: planning a sequel to *A Christmas Carol*.

- Re-read some pages from Stave One which are typical of Dickens' writing, for example, when Scrooge and Bob near the end of the working day. Focus on events, dialogue, the description of them finishing and leaving the office, and how the two behave immediately afterwards. Point out: long, complex sentences, sophisticated punctuation, descriptive detail, references to place and season, varied characters, contrast, Victorian vocabulary, strong atmosphere, realistic dialogue and precise punctuation.

- Investigate *A Christmas Carol* together. Ask: *How is the text divided? Do staves usually end at an interesting point?* Suggest that Dickens finishes a stave with important questions unanswered: the reader is drawn on.

- Return the children's 'Story planning' sheets from the previous activity. Let them use their notes to tell their story outline to a partner.

- Allocate time for the children to write the story, and suggest they consider a target length and add it to their notes.

- Allow the children to write their stories. Once complete, suggest peer and group review.

> **Differentiation**
> **Support:** Encourage children to work in groups of up to five and share the writing, each developing one section or chapter.
>
> ---
>
> **Extension:** Invite children to consider introducing stronger fear, ghostly appearances and stave headings.

Notes

- Use the notes below to help you to write two paragraphs about Christmas in Victorian times.

Victorian people made Christmas an important celebration

family members thought it important to get together

new Christmas traditions were begun by the Victorians

Prince Albert brought the tradition of decorating a tree from his native country Germany

people hung simple gifts for one another (fruits, sweets, nuts and handmade items) on the tree

in 1848 a magazine published a picture of Albert, Queen Victoria and their children with a Christmas tree, which ordinary people copied

presents grew larger and more expensive, so were placed under the tree

in 1843 Henry Cole had a card made to send to people at Christmas; other wealthy families started to do the same

Victorian children started making cards

Christmas dinner was an important occasion to share with your family

some people had goose or beef to eat, but turkey became the most popular meat for Christmas Day

Christmas crackers – invented by Tom Smith – were placed on the table

early Victorian mince pies contained meat; later ones, like ours, were sweet with dried fruit

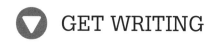

Creating an ending

● Make notes to help you plan a new ending for *A Christmas Carol*.

1. Does Scrooge really change his behaviour on Christmas morning? Are the Ghosts convinced?

_____

_____

_____

2. Is Bob Cratchit still poor? Does he need to wear his comforter now?

_____

_____

_____

3. Has Mrs Cratchit changed her attitude to Scrooge? What happens to Tiny Tim?

_____

_____

_____

4. Does Fred still want to mix with Scrooge? How does Fred's wife feel about Scrooge visiting them?

_____

_____

_____

5. Do people laugh at Scrooge? Maybe they think his new behaviour is false.

_____

_____

_____

6. Does Scrooge make more friends? Is he a happier man now?

_____

_____

_____

Other ideas I plan to include:

_____

_____

_____

 Story planning

● Use the planning frame below to help you develop a sequel to *A Christmas Carol*.

1. Opening

(Where? When? Who?) _____

_____

_____

2. Incidents

(What is the problem?
Is something miserly done?
Are cruel words said?)

_____

_____

3. Complications and dilemmas

(Who has a ghostly visit?
What does the ghost reveal? What
actions does the ghost demand?)

_____

_____

4. Resolution

(Is the problem solved? Is a wise decision made?)

_____

_____

5. Ending

(What is the final result? Is there a happy ending?)

_____

_____

ASSESSMENT ▶

1. Using hyphens

> **Objective**
> To use hyphens to avoid ambiguity.
> **What you need**
> Copies of *A Christmas Carol*.

What to do

- After reading Stave One, direct the children to the early pages of Stave One. Point out and write on the whiteboard: 'tight-fisted' and 'counting-house'. Ask: *What is the punctuation mark?* (hyphen) Ask: *How does a hyphen differ from a dash?* Show in nearby examples in the text that a hyphen is shorter than a dash.

- Explain that a hyphen can be used to join two words into one idea, for example, 'computer-mad', 'never-thinking'. It can also avoid confusion and make clear what word is being used, for example, 're-press' means 'to press again'; 'repress' means 'to hold things in'.

- Display this text on the whiteboard: 'Many of the Cratchits' worn out possessions were in need of some attention. One day Mrs Cratchit began work on a moth eaten chair. She would recover it! All it needed was an eye pleasing pattern of soothing colours. A better qualified upholsterer could have done this easily. It was back breaking work. After re pressing the material, Mrs Cratchit used a two hundred year old chain stitch sewing machine to create the cover. The finished result was certainly eye catching. The tightly pulled stitches looked terrible!' Ask the children to make the text's meaning clearer by rewriting it with hyphens.

> **Differentiation**
> **Support:** Let children read the text to each other before they write.
>
> **Extension:** Invite children to identify other hyphenated words in Stave One. Can they think of examples of their own?

2. Understanding words

> **Objective**
> To explore the meaning of words in context.
> **What you need**
> Copies of *A Christmas Carol*, dictionaries.
> **Cross curricular link**
> History

What to do

- After reading Stave Three, remind the children of the serving of the Cratchits' goose. Write this on the whiteboard: '...one murmur of delight arose all round the board'. Ask the children to discuss the meaning of 'board'. Agree and write a replacement word, for example 'table'.

- Write this on the whiteboard: 'The child had a small board on which to write his letters.' Ask the children to discuss the meaning of board here. Agree and write a replacement, for example 'piece of wood'. Ask: *Why is 'board' defined differently?* (different context) Explain that a word may have multiple meanings. Look up 'board' in a dictionary and find alternative meanings.

- Remind the children that *A Christmas Carol* was written in Victorian times. The language used at that time was often more formal and difficult than the language we use today. List these words on the whiteboard: 'prodigiously', 'plume', 'demeanour', 'aught', 'dogged', 'intricate', 'facetious', 'capacious', 'apprehensive', 'spontaneous'. Identify them as words from the first ten pages of Stave Three. The children must find each word, copy the phrase containing it, underline the word and write a replacement word or phrase of the same meaning.

> **Differentiation**
> **Extension:** Let the children repeat the activity with vocabulary from the stave's later pages.

3. Appropriate language

Objective
To distinguish between the language of speech and writing and choose the appropriate register.

What you need
Copies of *A Christmas Carol*.

Cross curricular link
History

What to do

- Read aloud Stave Four's three opening paragraphs. Comment on Dickens' complete sentences, precise punctuation, formal vocabulary, subject and verb agreement, full word forms rather than contractions. Progress to the scene in the beetling shop. Read aloud some of the dialogue. Comment on Dickens' informal style ('What odds, then?'), mistakes in subject and verb agreement ('if you was afraid'), incorrect grammar ('ever was spoke'), casual contractions ('em').

- Introduce the word 'register'. (Registers are the varieties of a language, shown through differences of vocabulary and grammar.) Comment that the encounter in the beetling shop is a situation when Dickens changes his register. Ask: *Do you think the grammar and vocabulary used here are appropriate? Why?*

- Ask the children to invent details for one of the women's stories about another victim. Share ideas: a rich lady had gold rings; her wigs were valuable; she treated servants harshly; she died friendless; items were stolen.

- Ask pairs to take turns being the charwoman or the laundress, telling the story to the owner of the beetling shop. They should then each write a few lines of the woman's new speech before assessing each other's written language and the appropriateness of its register.

Differentiation
Support: Remind children of register aspects to consider. Listen to oral work and accept less writing.

Extension: Expect more writing and greater awareness of how to vary a language's register.

4. Christmas spirit

Objective
To identify and discuss themes and conventions across a wide range of writing.

What you need
Copies of *A Christmas Carol*, photocopiable page 47 'Christmas spirit'.

Cross curricular link
Art and design

What to do

- Use this activity after finishing the book.

- Comment that the story's theme is Christmas. Point out that events occur on Christmas Eve and Christmas Day, and characters are involved with Christmas traditions. Suggest that the writer's aim is to remind the reader of the spirit of Christmas.

- Write the phrase 'the spirit of Christmas' on the whiteboard. Ask: *What does it mean?* Discuss answers and agree that it means being involved willingly and generously in Christmas traditions and celebrations.

- Underline 'spirit' on the whiteboard. Ask: *What other meaning does it have in this book?* (ghost)

- Direct the children to Stave Three when the second spirit allows Scrooge to see Christmas in Fred's house. Ask: *How does Scrooge change as he listens and watches? What is Dickens teaching the reader about Christmas spirit?* (Christmas is a time for family, fun and forgiveness.)

- Give out individual copies of photocopiable page 47 'Christmas spirit' for the children to complete independently. They should draw or write what Scrooge is taken to see or hear by a spirit, then describe how Scrooge reacts. They then write an explanation of the lesson Dickens is teaching the reader about Christmas spirit for each scene.

Differentiation
Support: Identify relevant text and encourage partner discussion before children complete the photocopiable page independently.

Extension: Ask children to identify more scenes where Dickens teaches us about Christmas spirit.

5. Awake or dreaming?

Objective
To note and develop initial ideas.

What you need
Copies of *A Christmas Carol*.

What to do

- Use this activity after finishing the book. When posing the questions suggested here, ask the children to make notes as they go along before progressing to whole-class exchanges.

- Suggest that the events of Christmas Eve night may not really happen: Scrooge could be dreaming.

- Revise Scrooge's Christmas Eve day contacts: his nephew, the two gentlemen, his clerk, the carol singer. Ask: *How does Scrooge behave with them?* Comment on his increasing irritability and rudeness.

- Indicate the description 'melancholy dinner' and the dull reading matter of his banker's book. Ask: *What is unsettling about his journey home?* (Fog and darkness make Scrooge struggle to find his way across the yard.)

- Read aloud the description of Marley's face on the door knocker. Ask: *What effect does it have on Scrooge? How does he change his usual behaviour in the house?* Point out his pause, cautious checks and double-locking.

- Suggest that by the time Scrooge sits by the fire and then goes to bed, he must be agitated. Ask: *Did his food disagree with him? Is he feeling guilty about his earlier brusque, uncharitable behaviour?*

- Write this question on the whiteboard: 'Is Scrooge's night a dream or real?' Suggest that the children consult the notes they have made and decide what they think, before writing a preliminary draft and final piece. Emphasise the value of including relevant references to the text.

Differentiation

Support: Encourage further discussion in pairs and offer adult support with notes.

Extension: Expect more perceptive analysis and original viewpoints.

6. Recommending books

Objective
To recommend books that they have read to their peers, giving reasons for their choices.

What you need
Copies of *A Christmas Carol*.

Cross curricular link
History

What to do

- Do this activity after finishing the book.

- Explain that you will be reading *A Christmas Carol* with next year's class. You would like your new children to be enthusiastic about the book before starting it. Recommendations from children in this year's class would be useful.

- Use partner and then class discussion to share positive comments, for example, the story holds the reader's interest; the main character is unusual; Victorian London is an interesting setting.

- Emphasise that you want the children to speak, not read, their recommendations. Suggest that cue cards would remind them what to say next.

- Give an A4 piece of paper or card to each child for them to make their five cue cards. The content of each cue card should be brief and clear: notes or sketches to remind them what to say.

- After preparing their cue cards, let the children practise their speaking with partners. Organise listening groups, so that everyone experiences speaking to a group.

- Arrange a visit from next year's class, so that the children can make their recommendations to a visiting partner.

Differentiation

Support: Allow partners to work together on their cue cards and oral recommendation, each speaking for some of the time.

Extension: Expect children to speak at greater length and to provide sound justification for their opinions.

Christmas spirit

- Using the relevant pages in the book to help you, complete each section of the table below.

	What the spirit lets Scrooge see or hear	How Scrooge reacts	What Dickens teaches us about the spirit of Christmas
In Stave Two, the spirit takes Scrooge to a schoolroom.			
In Stave Two, the spirit takes Scrooge to Mr Fezziwig's office.			
In Stave Three, the spirit takes Scrooge to Bob Cratchit's house.			

SCHOLASTIC

Available in this series:

978-1407-16055-9

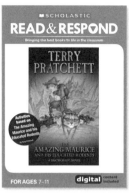

978-1407-16056-6

978-1407-16057-3

978-1407-16058-0

978-1407-16059-7

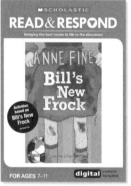

978-1407-16060-3

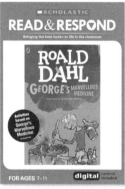

978-1407-16061-0

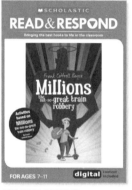

978-1407-16062-7

978-1407-16063-4

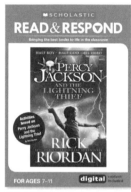

978-1407-16064-1

978-1407-16065-8

978-1407-16052-8

978-1407-16067-2

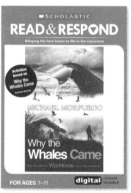

978-1407-16068-9

978-1407-16069-6

978-1407-16070-2

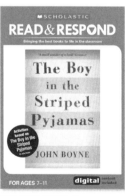

978-1407-16071-9

978-1407-17616-1

978-1407-17614-7

978-1407-17615-4

To find out more, call: 0845 6039091
or visit our website www.scholastic.co.uk/readandrespond